PIANO • VOCAL • GUITAR

KANSAS
GREATEST HITS

Cover photo © Jeffrey Mayer

ISBN 978-1-4234-3769-7

HAL•LEONARD®
CORPORATION
7777 W. BLUEMOUND RD. P.O. BOX 13819 MILWAUKEE, WI 53213

Visit Hal Leonard Online at
www.halleonard.com

ALL I WANTED

Words and Music by STEVE WALSH
and STEVE MORSE

Moderately, with a steady beat

You say _____ it's
There's no need for
It's not _____ so

time to stay _____ be-hind.
blame 'cause we're not the same.
strange for us _____ to change. _____

All I want-ed was to hold you. _____
All I want-ed was to love you. _____
All I want-ed was to touch you. _____

CARRY ON WAYWARD SON

Words and Music by
KERRY LIVGREN

FIGHT FIRE WITH FIRE

Words and Music by JOHN ELEFANTE
and DINO ELEFANTE

13

DUST IN THE WIND

Words and Music by
KERRY LIVGREN

Moderate Folk style

HOLD ON

Words and Music by
KERRY LIVGREN

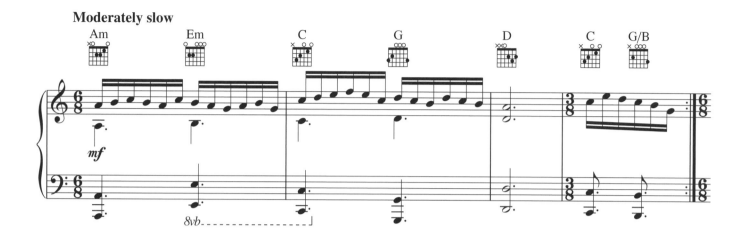

Look in the mir-ror and tell me just what you see.
Don't you re-call what you felt when you weren't a-lone?
Out-side your door he is wait-ing, wait-ing for you.

What have the years of your life taught you to be?
Some-one who stood by your side, a face you have known?
Soon-er or lat-er you know he's got to come through.

NO ONE TOGETHER

Words and Music by
KERRY LIVGREN

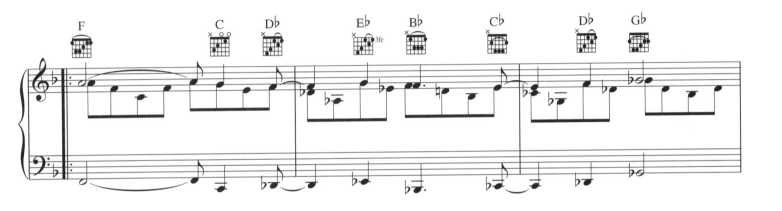

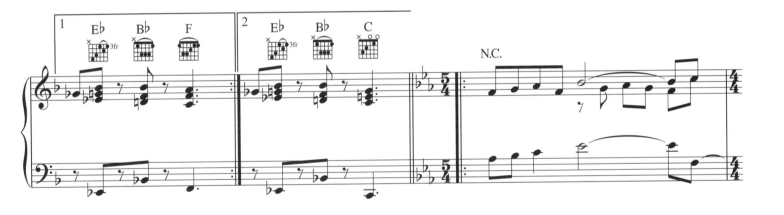

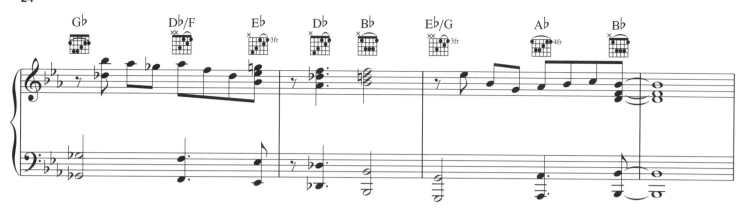

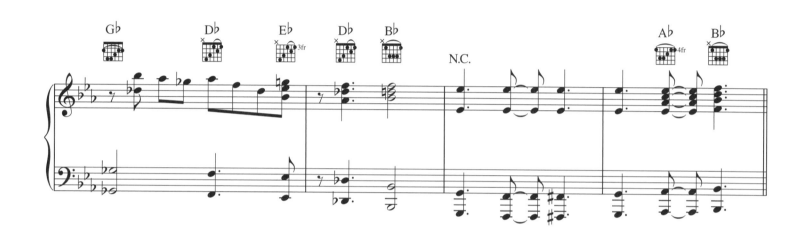

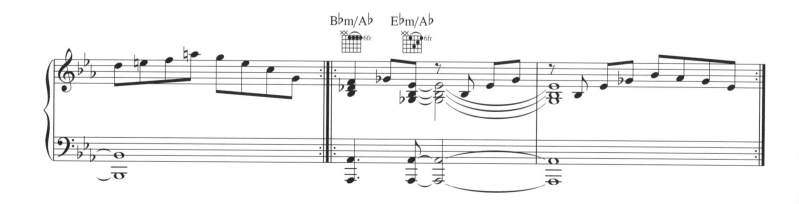

1. Cen - tu - ries ___ of back - ward ways ___ have
2. Lo, the horn ___ of plen - ty ___ is
(3.) mul - ti - tudes ___ are search - ing ___ and

man - y left ___ be - hind ___ us ___ who can count ___ the good ___
burst-ing at ___ the seam. ___ The har - vest of ___ the world ___
won-der - ing ___ in vain, ___ for what they seek ___ can - not ___

3. The

D.S. al Coda

CODA

Ev - 'ry - one ___ is me ___ and   you. ___

(Vocal 1st time only)

8vb

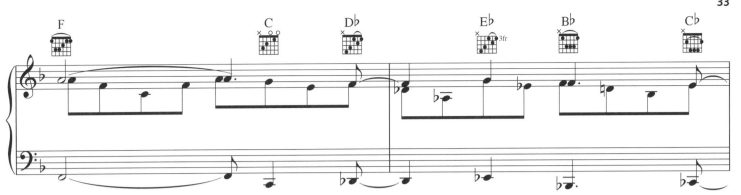

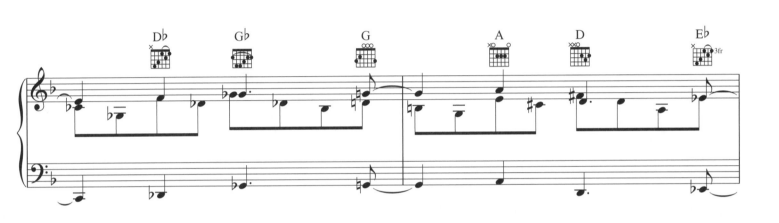

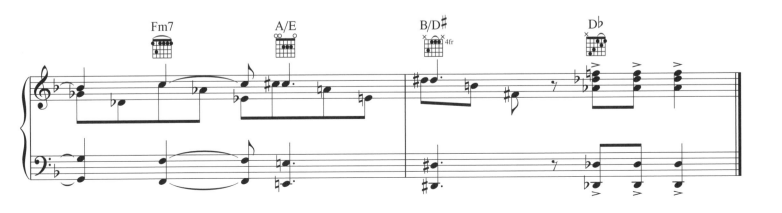

ICARUS
(Borne on Wings of Steel)

Words and Music by
KERRY LIVGREN

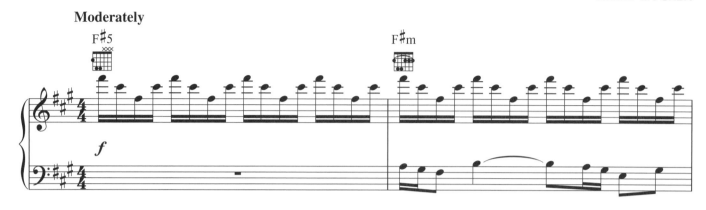

Ear - ly in the morn - ing sun - light,
High - er than the birds, I'm fly - ing.
Dawn - ing on the clouds of am - ber,

PLAY THE GAME TONIGHT

Words and Music by KERRY LIVGREN,
PHIL EHART, RICHARD WILLIAMS,
DANNY FLOWER and ROBERT FRAZIER

You think that some - thin's _ hap - p'nin', ___ that it's
And when the cur - tains o - pen ___ to the

big - ger than _ your life, ____ but it's on - ly ___ what you're
roar - ing of _ the crowd, ___ you will feel it ___ all a -

hear - ing.
round ___ you. ____

Will you
Then it

POINT OF KNOW RETURN

Words and Music by STEVE WALSH, PHIL EHART
and ROBERT STEINHARDT

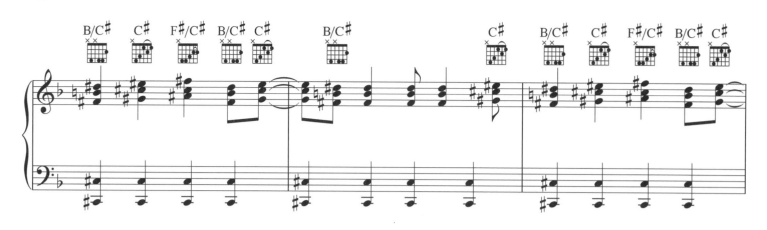

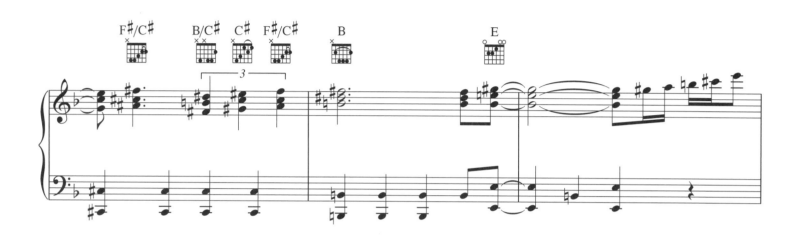

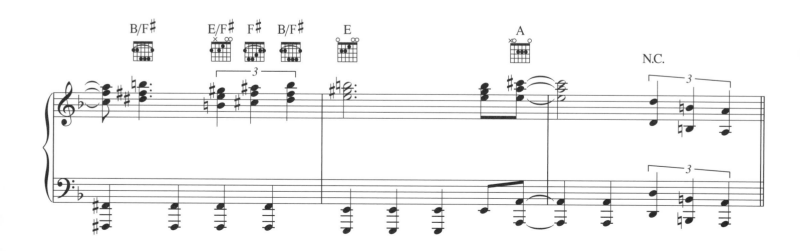

PORTRAIT
(He Knew)

Words and Music by KERRY LIVGREN
and STEVE WALSH

Moderately slow, in 2

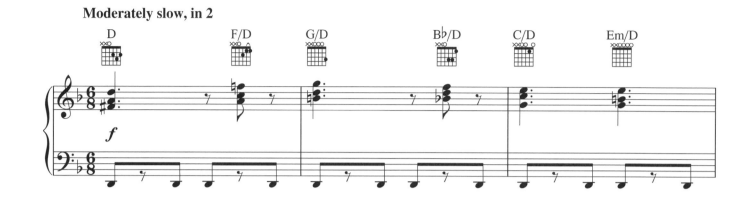

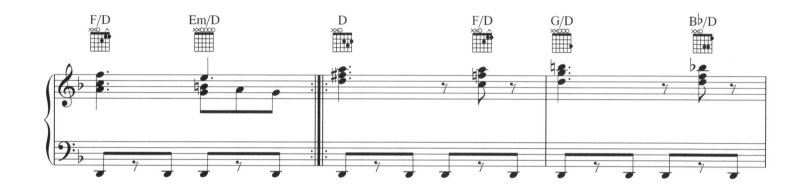

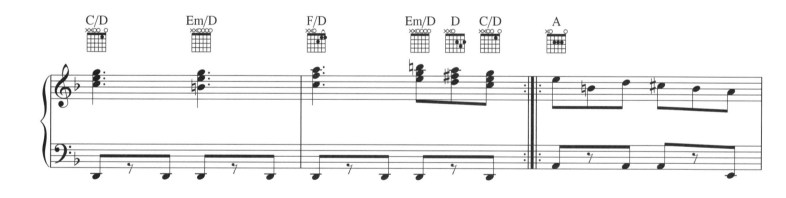

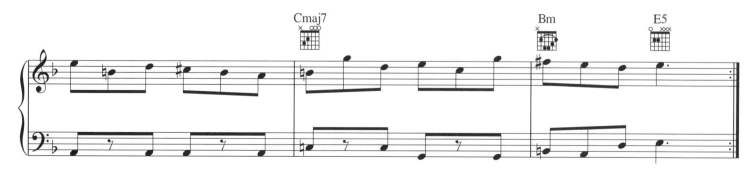

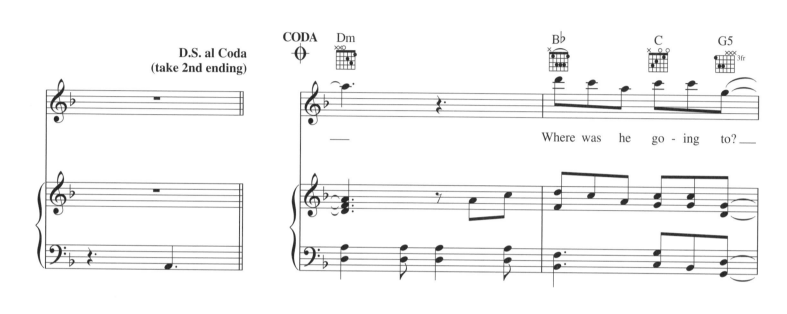

D.S. al Coda
(take 2nd ending)

CODA

Where was he go - ing to?

Very fast

THE WALL

Words and Music by KERRY LIVGREN
and STEVE WALSH

SONG FOR AMERICA

Words and Music by
KERRY LIVGREN

Medium Rock beat

Vir - gin land __ of __ for - est green, __
Paint - ed des - ert, se - quined sky, __
High - ways sear __ the moun - tain sides, __